THE *James River Plantations* COOKBOOK

TEXT BY

Payne Bouknight Tyler

PRODUCED BY

Winston B. Spurgeon

PHOTOGRAPHY BY

Charles Jordan Joanne Jordan

CULINARY EXPERT

Vincent H. Petraglia

DESIGN BY

Kathryn A. Berry

— Our Special Appreciation To —

The Colonial Williamsburg Foundation, Mr. & Mrs. Harrison Ruffin Tyler, Mrs. Walter O. Major, Mrs. Bradley H. Gunter, Mr. & Mrs. Frederick Fisher, Westover Church, Mr. & Mrs. Malcolm Jamieson, Mr. & Mrs. Charles Hill Carter, Jr., Congressman Robert W. Daniel, Jr., Miss Harriet Carter, Mrs. William Bouknight, Mrs. Armistead H. Boyd, Mrs. Pleasants Bagby, Mr. Al Vazquez

"Sunny Day," Graphic Arts Department

Williamsburg
Publishing Co.
P.O. Box 1865, Williamsburg, Va. 23185

The James River

Fields and Plantation houses, representing a timeless way of life, grace the shoreline of the James River.

The heart of plantation life was, and still is, the James River. This powerful waterway has its Virginia beginnings in the Appalachian Mountains. It flows through the Piedmont, past the coastal plain of Tidewater, and empties its strength into the Chesapeake Bay. Its upper reaches are rocky and filled with rapids near the Falls (established by Colonel William Byrd in 1742 as a trading post called Richmond). From this point toward the ocean, the James develops into a highly navigable waterway. On the north side its banks can reach ninety feet, and on the south side they frequently drop to water level. Cypress trees line its shores. Their protruding knees make navigation near the shore line difficult, while their bark and the droppings from their branches cause the darkness of color that is so prominent in its local tributaries.

Creeks bearing the names of Mapsico, Tomahond, Kittiewan, and Tappanhanna contribute to its confluence. Plantations established for centuries face the fast moving waters, and local places named The Curles, Weyanoke, Teddington, and The Rowe, blend with the better known plantations of Belle Air, Berkeley, Westover, Sherwood Forest, Shirley, Brandon, and Carter's Grove.

First known to man as the Powhatan, the James, named to honor the English King, was the early highway of Tidewater, Virginia. It was at Sandy Point that the Indian werowance, Powhatan, Father of the Princess Pocahontas, established his town of Paspahegh, the seat of one of the most powerful confederations in Virginia, and evidences of the contributions of this civilization are intermingled today into the lives of the peoples of Charles City.

My husband and children are direct descendants of Powhatan. So are a large number of other residents of this county. It would be difficult to find a family with a

Charles City background of several hundred years whose ancestors were not, at some point, closely connected with our county's first inhabitants.

We frequently spend our Sunday afternoons on the James, where the waters rise and fall four feet each twelve hours. Picnic Day: the boat, loaded with children and deviled crab, dogs and water skis, is usually piloted by a competent teen-ager, whose knowledge of tides and currents exceeds the scope of the average adult.

We search for beaches — the tide must drop to uncover the sand, so our trips are planned accordingly. Our favorite used to be at Dancing Point, where Colonel Philip Lightfoot danced with the Devil around a burning tree stump by light of the full moon. We now go to Flowerdieu Hundred, with beaches wide and sandy, where at one time flourished the Indian Village of Weyanoke.

Cypress trees dot the shoreline along the James. County residents refer to them as "water magnolias," because, when seen from a distance, the herons which nest there appear to be blossoms.

As evening comes, we steer for our own beach — past houses of river fishermen and remnants of steam boat docks, reminders of a distant method of 19th century river transportation.

We tie to our weathered dock, and here we have cocktails and prepare seafood — some local, some from nearby fish houses. After dinner, when the sun is out of sight and the muddy James turns dark blue, we pack and return to Sherwood Forest. We leave the James, the heart of the County of Charles City.

Charles City County

The political units in early Virginia were at first separate settlements, variously called cities, towns, plantations and hundreds, a concept of land which was designed to contain one hundred families. The settlers were primarily people of non-agrarian background, and they anticipated that society would develop in this new country as it had in England. The cultivation of tobacco, the stimulus for the beginnings of the great James River Plantations, provoked separation and isolation. Society became, from the first, distinctly agricultural and rural. As a result, there is today no city in Charles City County.

In 1616, Charles City was patented as Smith's Hundred. Within six years, the struggling county was almost devastated by a planned attack of Indians upon settlers, the Indian Massacre of 1622. Reestablishment was necessary. In 1634 the colony of Virginia was divided into eight shires. With the exception of two, all of these were situated on the James River. The Shire of Charles City extended on both sides of the river; on the south side from Lawne's Creek to Chippokes Creek, and on the north side from Skiffe's Creek to above Sandy Point or Paspahegh.

Immense individual holdings of land began to appear, and the economic stability of Charles City was established on a definite agricultural basis. Peoples were imported to the area for the cultivation of land. Ships were built to carry products across oceans for trade. Houses were constructed, added to, and enlarged. Dependencies for the various activities of country life were created: smokehouses, tobacco barns, stables, ice houses, kitchens, carriage houses, milk houses, and necessary houses. The beginnings of life on the great plantations of the James River had become established, and in the course of more than three hundred years the plantations have held their own — through three wars fought on their soil with armed troops encamped on grounds and in drawing rooms, with a graciousness of habitation that is unique to no other part of America.

As a resident of Charles City, I appreciate its uniqueness, yet my viewpoint at times tends to veer in the direction of the visitor — the person who immediately sees the archaic structure of this environmental concept. I was not born here, yet my love for this county and its peoples has become deeply entrenched. It gives me pleasure to hear spoken today, words that ring of pure old English pronunciation, to see the working peoples who were born in this county dance the steps of a dance that is straight from Medieval England. Yet I know that they are unaware of their special charm.

It is through activity that Charles City's atmosphere is preserved. It is through contentment, but not complacency, that this way of life is maintained. Few children of the educated families spend their total childhood in this county. Preparatory schools and travel are their lot. College degrees are acquired from all sections of the United States and Europe, and graduate degrees are considered a necessary part of the development. Education is the basis upon which their appreciation for their county is stimulated. Constant effort and activity are the necessities for the maintenance of their chosen way of life.

Men from this county have served in every political capacity that our nation has had to offer. They have sacrificed their homes, and sons and families, to preserve a way of life, a particular unit of social form, a level of agrarian economy.

Today, not all activity is agricultural. The large plantations still function, crops are grown and harvested, houses are maintained and treasured, yet the man of the house, in all probability, has another occupation, sometimes with a commuting distance of seventy or so miles, and frequently with branches of his business distributed across our nation.

Charles City is the area known as the cradle of the Republic. The leaders of early Virginia, consequently our early nation, were born, lived, and died here. Its residents always return. A Harrison, from Berkeley, drove by carriage from Ohio to write his inaugural address, for the Presidency, in the room in which he was born. Charles City, the county with no city, is a very special place, a county of pride, of enchantment, and of accomplishment. It stands alone as a personal survivor of an era long past, a progenitor of a way of life unchanged, and a contributor to a unique and specialized part of the life of America.

Tranquil Herring Creek becomes a center of local activity in the Spring. The herring return here every season to spawn, and are so plentiful that they can be scooped up in nets and buckets.

Carter's Grove

One of the truly great plantations along the James is Carter's Grove, located in James City County. Today, visitors to this house approach the 18th century plantation along a placid, country road reminiscent of the days when early Virginia aristocrats sought hospitality and congenial company at the elegant James River estates.

One passes through primitive woodlands, pastures, marshes and streams; one sees local cardinals and geese that fly in for the season; and at the termination of this road is the stately mansion which was built by Carter Burwell in the mid 1750's. Seventeen hundred and eighty acres of the original tract, bought by King Carter for his daughter, Elizabeth, and given to her as a wedding gift, still surround this house. Carter's will specified that this particular plantation should pass to Elizabeth's son, Carter Burwell, and that, "in all times to come be called and go by the name of Carter's Grove." For nearly a century the Burwell family occupied this property which subsequently passed through a succession of owners until it was purchased by Rockefeller interests in 1963.

Two of the most memorable owners were Mr. and Mrs. Archibald McCrea, who lived at Carter's Grove for forty years. The McCreas devoted time and energy to Carter's Grove — and contributed much toward the proper restoration of the house. They joined the flanking office building to the central house, improved upon an earlier connection between the house and kitchen building, and they also added dormer windows.

Entertainment in the 20th century — following the Virginia pattern established for the previous 200 years — was of a high order. Many notable and influential guests visited Carter's Grove. As late as 1936 President Franklin D. Roosevelt was entertained at this estate.

Shortly after our marriage, Harrison announced that we were driving to a place below Williamsburg to have tea with one of his mother's friends. This was Mrs. McCrea, a delightful person who entertained us with stories of Carter's Grove. She told us of the Refusal Room — one of the very formal drawing rooms, where legend projects the concept that both George Washington and Thomas Jefferson were rejected in their proposals of marriage by two Virginia belles. It was here that Mary Cary decided not to marry Washington, and Rebecca Burwell, the young and charming niece of Carter Burwell, who was known locally as "Fair Belinda," refused Jefferson.

I found particularly fascinating the story of how Banastre Tarleton, Colonel of the British Army during the Revolutionary War, rode his horse up the wide stairs, slashing the bannister railing with his sword. Tarleton left the scars of this fruitless and somewhat romantic endeavor to be seen by future generations.

The architectural detail of Carter's Grove is among the finest in America. The

The upper hall of Carter's Grove is an excellent example of the magnificent paneling throughout the house. This is accented by meticulously hand-carved detail.

— opposite —
The dining room table at Carter's Grove is set with a succulent Virginia Ham* in the foreground. Featured clockwise are Quail, Cranberry Aspic, Spinach Ring, Spoon Bread* and Meat Pasties.

— below —
Although elegant, the library at Carter's Grove is warm and comfortable.

entrance hall and staircase are noted for their beauty of proportion and for their unusual paneling and carved woodwork. Architectural historian Thomas Waterman wrote of Carter's Grove:

> "The great suite of paneled rooms on the river front is the glory of Carter's Grove and is as fine as any other in the country. The entrance salon to the south, with its adjoining stair hall, is one of the outstanding examples of American woodwork . . . The stair ascends in a long initial flight on the west wall, then turns in two short flights before reaching the second floor. Great attention was lavished on the detail of the stair, even the dowels that fix the walnut nosings to the stair tread being covered with plugs in the form of Fleur-de-lis."

Today Carter's Grove is owned by The Colonial Williamsburg Foundation. It adds a major dimension to the overall historic interpretation of colonial history in the Tidewater area.

Sherwood Forest

Wrought iron gates and Empire pillars lead the visitor toward Sherwood Forest. This carriage entrance was designed by President John Tyler in 1845. It is bordered by trees that were in existence when Indians occupied this area, when Revolutionary troops passed along its borders, and when Union generals McClellan, Butterfield and Butler camped beneath these same branches. A remarkable white house, the longest frame house in America, completely overpowers the end of the avenue. It is surrounded by 12 acres of lawn, and its 300 foot length is emphasized by the linear placement of its original dependencies: smokehouse, wine house, necessary house and milk house (all in one endless progression). Boxwood and magnolias, planted before the Revolutionary War, are dwarfed by the remarkable size of this elegant but simple house.

This is Sherwood Forest, the home of the 10th President of the United States, a man whose family has resided in Virginia long enough to know that they sold their Middle Plantation for the site of the City of Williamsburg. John Tyler was the fourth generation in Virginia to bear the same name, practice law, engage in politics, and live the life of a country planter. For centuries to the present day, his family has held public office: Governors of Virginia, Vice-Lords of the Admiralty Court, Federal Judges, Chancellors and Presidents of the College of William and Mary, United States Senators, and state and federal Congressional Representatives.

Sherwood Forest is a very personal house — it is filled with the furniture, porcelains and paintings of John Tyler and his family. Its colors and wallpaper are the ones chosen by his wife, Julia Gardiner. Its carriage lamps on the north porch lighted the President's carriage, and the iron Chesapeake retrievers that guard its entrance were wedding presents to John Tyler and Julia Gardiner. This house is fascinating because it is the architectural expression of two articulate individuals — a house built in 1730, and altered in 1845, to meet the demands of the aesthetic but practical concepts of two educated and worldly people.

In Sherwood's 68 foot ballroom, the 10th President of the United States danced the Virginia Reel, and he entertained the renowned of two continents with his own violin compositions. In its drawing room, with its gold leaf architectural embellishments by the New York architect, LaFever, Tyler tacked wooden weather-stripping to the doors, an act which prompted his wife to record, "The President is an excellent politician, but a very mediocre carpenter." And over the entire 1600 acre working plantation, still farmed and lived in by his great-grandchildren, he created an atmosphere of home life and fatherly devotion. Tyler was the father of fifteen children, and evidences of his family's 150 year residence at Sherwood Forest are everywhere.

My husband, Harrison, is a grandson of John Tyler. In three centuries, there have been only three generations within his particular family line. Today Sherwood Forest is very much our home. Our children are now with us only sporadically. I miss the sounds of motor-bikes dashing up the avenue where carriages used to pass, and the voices of children getting up for an early morning's hunt. But change is inevitable, progress necessary, and education vital. Our immediate family is scattered over two continents, acquiring the background and knowledge to enable them to cope with today's world.

We travel regularly — but the best part of the trip is looking forward to coming home. Are the leaves out? Are the horses fed? I like living at Sherwood Forest. I know as I go about the everyday business of plantation management — crops in the field, hay for the cattle, balancing the accounts — that our parents, grandparents, and great-grandparents have enjoyed many of the same things that give us pleasure today: a good dessert of apple float, a swim in the Goose Pond, a venison dinner on Oriental Export, communion with a Healy portrait, a cool glass of buttermilk.

Today the ornate openwork of this 18th century dairy is aesthetically pleasing. In colonial times it encouraged a necessary circulation of air.

Christmas Day at Sherwood is important. It is at this season that the family comes. Cars drive through the snow and certain predictable cousins park on the lawn instead of in the parking areas. Children hitch "Dilapidated Pony" to the snow cart while others drag or ride behind, and some undisciplined teenager may sneak a shot at a goose left behind on the fishing pond.

Everybody contributes to the Christmas Dinner at Sherwood. Our table is covered with a cloth of Point de France, a memento of someone's 19th century travels abroad. It is usually set with Rose Medallion — a gift to Harrison's grandfather from the Emperor of China — and country ham, watermelon pickle, candied sweet potatoes and Sally Lunn are staples. Ambrosia, fruit cake, Charlotte Russe, and pound cake are our Christmas desserts. These are preceded by a good, chilled, Mint Julep.

— opposite —
Christmas today at Sherwood Forest is much the same as it was for President Tyler. Roast Suckling Pig,* Sally Lunn,* Stuffed Tomatoes,* Creamed Spinach, Watermelon Pickle, Glazed Country Ham,* and Candied Sweet Potatoes* are still enjoyed.

— below —
The South Porch at Sherwood Forest faced the original entrance to the Plantation. It was here that President Tyler enjoyed his afternoon Juleps.

Belle Air

East of Charles City Courthouse and on the left, as one goes toward Williamsburg, lies "Belle Air." Built in the 17th century, on the most prominent elevation of Colonel Thomas Stegge's 1700 acre plantation, this frame house has survived for over 300 years. The home is modest, but elegant for its period. It was built circa 1650 to 1670, and was named "Belle Air" by 18th century owners. The "beautiful site" commands a full view of the surrounding 200 acres of cultivated farmland with pine forests beyond.

Belle Air has been the home of Mrs. Walter O. Major since the 1950's, when she and her late husband saved the long neglected structure from ruin. Together they restored it to a thoroughly livable, yet very important, architectural landmark.

The 17th century house exemplifies the earliest form of colonial construction, with a center hall up and down, which is flanked by rooms to the east and west. Probably built by shipwrights, it is one of the few remaining homes in America which contains the original Jacobean period framing. Easily recognizable are the huge architectural summer beams and chimney girts, which are directly connected into the chimneys of both the great hall and library. Vertical corner and intermediate posts, decorated with chamfered edges and lamb's-tongue groove, are mortised into the exposed sills. These complete the striking use of structure as decorative trim. Such hearty decor is absent in the more refined 18th century addition, which is beyond the west chimney.

The six foot wide center hall is made majestic by its closed stringer Jacobean stair. Completely original, with string balusters carved from native heart pine, it is akin to medieval woodwork. It is considered the solitary example of a 17th century balustrade in Virginia.

In the dining room at Belle Air is a two hundred year old banquet table of walnut which was made in our county of Charles City by local craftsmen. Like most of the family heirlooms in the house, it is in constant use. Meriwether Major's table is set with Chinese Canton, and her centerpiece is often the combination of early 19th century sandwich glass candlesticks which rest on either side of an antique ivory figurine. These Meri surrounds with sprigs of a rare English ivy, its leaf a miniature which she also enjoys as a garnish.

Near the smokehouse, and adjacent to the old kitchen, is the herb garden, one of the most enchanting features at Belle Air. This was designed and planted by Meri, an authority on herbs, their horticulture, harvesting, and culinary use. Her parsley and chive butter to be spread on homemade bread is so easy to prepare, and her herb-seasoned broiled flounder is not to be missed.

Meri comes from a long line of the finest cooks and hostesses in Virginia and she is fortunate to be able to raise her own vegetables. One summer, knowing she would be away for several weeks, she called to see if I would like to use her vegetables so they would continue to reproduce. It was a bounty of the best tomatoes, zucchini, peppers, and snaps — although we had torrential rains and I had to wear fishermen's boots in order to gather these crops for the table.

Belle Air's resonant dinner bell is used to summon hungry family and guests for dinner.

— above —
Meri Major, pictured here, is busy preparing a variety of Charles City delicacies —
Soft Shell Crabs,* Fried Chicken,* Broiled Fish,* and Pecan Pie.*

— opposite —
This eighteenth century walnut banquet table supports a bounty of delectable fare.
Herb Fish* is pictured in the foreground, homemade bread with Herb Butter,* Corn Pudding*
and Zucchini-Tomato Casserole.* The side table is shown with
Queen Anne Lace and Caramel Ginger Pie.*

— below —
Herbs and vegetables border this early Belle Air smokehouse, which served as a food vault
in early plantation life. The herb garden is adjacent to the old kitchen in the background.

— above —
A hearty Hunt Breakfast of Fried Salt Herring* and Roe, Sweet Rolls, Fried Apples, Eggs, Bacon, Blueberry Pancakes, Hominy Grits, Beef Tenderloin, and Fried Potatoes with Onions. This lavish meal is complemented by a hot Stirrup Cup of Coffee and Brandy

— opposite —
Governor Tyler's law practice prospered from this small law office building adjacent to his home.

Greenway was the home of Judge John Tyler, several times Governor of Virginia, Federal Judge, Vice-Lord of the Admiralty Courts, Revolutionary Captain, Chancellor of the College of William and Mary, attorney, planter, and father of John Tyler, 10th President of the United States.

His son, John Tyler, was born here. This, plus its enchanting design of the typical planter's home of early Virginia, gives the house its distinction. Its exterior is white clapboard; there is a center hall flanked by two rooms up and down, with a 19th century addition on the back. This was evidently constructed by a local carpenter, for the hand-carved sunburst mantel is identical to one on the second floor at Sherwood Forest.

The drawing room mantel is extremely handsome. Paneled walnut covers the entire chimney breast, and fluted pilasters support its sides.

Greenway is unique. All of its original 18th century dependencies are intact. The old kitchen, servant's house, and smokehouse are flanked by apple trees and boxwoods, the remains of an 18th century English garden. Directly opposite is Governor Tyler's law office, a small and charming structure where he practiced law and probably entertained his two closest freinds, Thomas Jefferson and Patrick Henry. At the back of the garden is his grave, above ground, slightly leaning to one side, and resting beneath an ancient and tilted tree.

At Greenway was bred Robert Waddell, thoroughbred winner of the first American Derby.

Hunt Breakfast, the meal enjoyed not before the hunt, but in mid-afternoon when the hunters have returned, has long been a staple in Charles City: hominy, cooked in milk and stirred with butter to make it creamy, herring caught during the season and smoked and salted for later use, and pancakes cooked on a griddle and served with local fruits. But most important is the Stirrup Cup — steaming black coffee spiked with straight brandy — the Hunter's Delight, and the backbone of a cold day.

Each spring Charles City residents and visitors anxiously await the annual run of shad. Featured here are, from left, Lemon Pie, Baked Shad, Homemade Bread, Cole Slaw* and Hush Puppies.*

Westover Church

High on the hillside of Herring Creek rests Westover Church. One of our monuments to the Episcopal heritage of early Virginia, this church has participated in every phase of Charles City's development since the early 1700's. Not only has it served as a religious center for the early parish of Westover, but during the two major wars fought on American soil, it has housed troops of the British General Cornwallis and the Union General McClellan.

The earliest tombstone in Westover's graveyard bears the date 1748. Others may be more ancient, but their inscriptions are now illegible. All of its graves, many of them housing the members of Virginia's earliest and most illustrious families for more than three centuries, rest in the shade of trees whose branches stretch upward and outward toward the marsh at Herring Creek.

The parish of Westover is scattered today, covering an area of thirty to forty miles of rural properties. Two hundred years ago, the Charles City communicants of this church numbered approximately the same as today, and a check into the minutes of the meetings of the church will reveal the fact that many of the supporting families of Westover Parish have not changed in two centuries — even the Christian names which precede the family names are the same.

Westover Church was built originally on the banks of the James, on the western side of Westover House. Before 1740, an excess of after-service visitors from a scattered parish prompted the wife of William Byrd II to take measures to protect herself from a situation of too strenuous entertainment. Therefore, the church was moved, brick by brick, across an especially constructed causeway which spanned the upper reaches of Herring Creek, an area of wide marsh and sloping banks.

The church structure is classic in its simplicity. Completely rectangular with a sharply canted roof, the 18th century construction boasts glazed headers and rubbed brick. The windows are arched and extend to the roofline. There is a small clerestory window, above the pedimented entrance door. This gives light to a balcony which originally was used as a seating space for the servants of the members of the church. The interior of Westover is white. A single aisle down the center leads to a semi-circular Communion rail. Beyond this, the nave is centered under an arched window, flanked by two entablatures, which contain the Ten Commandments.

When I first attended Westover, this window was always covered with climbing greens, frequently clematis, painstakingly and charmingly arranged by Eddie Brown, our Sexton. Harrison sat in the fourth pew from the front on the left: it is interesting to note that every Sunday the majority of communicants who enter Westover will take their places in the same seats that their families have occupied for generations.

The Women's Auxiliary of Westover Church is an active group. The pillow for the kneeling rail was designed and made by them. It beautifully expresses the simple country elegance of this church. Worked in needlepoint, it combines the religious symbols of the Christian Doctrine with the wildflowers of the county.

Garden week in Virginia is closely connected with this church, for it is here that the visitors to the area are served, by the ladies of Westover, a lunch of Brunswick Stew and Chicken Tetrazzini. The receipt for the Tetrazzini is closely guarded — but the stew has been for so long a staple of early Virginia that everyone knows the receipt. It is a combination of vegetables from the garden and local meats — always accented by squirrel. Its origin stems from the days when meat was brought home by hunters, Indians supplied the colonists with corn, and cooking was done in large quantities in iron pots over an open kitchen fire.

Westover

Westover Plantation justifies the description given it during the Revolutionary War by the Marquis de Castelleux, "The most beautiful house in America." From marble mantles to carved plaster ceilings, hand carved bannisters and paneled walls, its strength and beauty are overpowering. The architectural proportions of Westover are staggering; the main stair has steps that are five feet wide.

The broad and muddy James borders its grounds on the south side. On the north are the wrought iron gates of William Byrd II. These classic gates are flanked by ten-foot columns surmounted by sculptured eagles half the size of a man. The pediment over the gates is beautifully wrought, with the initials, W. B., interwoven into its design.

To the west of the house is a boxwood garden, formal in the English concept, with a brick fence enclosing it from the surrounding view. The design of this garden focuses on a marble obelisk — the grave of William Byrd II, a highly polished, educated, and entertaining man who wrote his own epitaph.

In the early 1700's, William Byrd II inherited property of 26,231 acres from his Father, William Byrd I, who had purchased the Westover land from Theodoric Bland, one of Charles City's progenitors. Between the years of 1726 and 1730, he constructed the house. His sense of the aesthetic was exquisite.

During the early settlement of Virginia, the educated landowners sent their sons

— left —
The inner gate
at Westover is flanked by massive
columns supporting beaufifully
detailed eagles, a symbol
of the Byrd name.

— below —
Legend relates that, after church,
William Byrd removed the top
from one of these decorative urns
and served punch to his guests.

to England for schooling and social development. Known as the "Black Swan," William Byrd was an excellent example of the sensibility of this order. His political contributions were many, he founded the cities of Richmond and Petersburg, his library was the best in Virginia, and his personal diary, recorded daily for years, reflects intimate details of the life of the Virginia planter. His personality was spirited; he loved women and music and rode frequently to hounds.

Westover Church originally stood near the Westover garden, close to the river. Local legend says that the congenial Byrd served punch after Sunday services, and many parishioners, as a result, stayed for weeks in the mansion as house guests. As a consequence, he dismantled the Church and moved it to its present site. This was accomplished by the building of a causeway almost one-half mile long, across Herring Creek. The causeway was then destroyed (one can see the remains today), forcing parishioners to make a trip of over four miles by carriage or horseback if they chose to visit Mrs. Byrd after Sunday services.

The "Black Swan" had many children, but the most remembered is his daughter, Evelyn, who died of a broken heart after being forbidden to marry the man she loved. Her grave, wrapped in iron bands, is visible today, near the river at Westover where the old church stood. Her spirit still remains, never having left the house of her childhood, and many are the people who have heard the physical sounds of her expression of woe.

During the 19th century, Westover had numerous owners. But the family that lives there today has occupied it for four generations. Under the trees where the "Black Swan" gambled at cards, drank homemade wine and ate Westover Crackers, one finds today a set of children's swings, the modern embellishments of today's world. Fred and Muschi Fisher, and their small children have come to live at Westover, where Fred lived as a child. His mother, Bruce Crane Fisher, daughter of Richard Crane, former Minister to Czechoslovakia, has recently vacated the house, thus ending a particular era of generosity, kindness, and affection that the residents of our county will not forget.

My first visit to Westover was after morning service at Westover church — the tradition still lingers. Bruce had asked Harrison and me to join her for wine and Westover Crackers. It was a spring day and buttercups were on the lawn. We sat, facing the James, in rustic chairs made of local trees. We were served wine and crackers, round, flat and brittle and soon the buttercups were joined by cracker crumbs — for it is impossible to eat these crackers without their crumbling. And whenever they are served, on Bruce's flat silver plate, in the garden or in the drawing room, one endures the crumbs, for Westover Crackers are the perfect accompaniment to our local wines.

— opposite —
Westover's grace is reflected
in this simple setting on the front
lawn. A glass of local wine accompanies
the Westover Crackers,* which have
been enjoyed here for generations.

Berkeley

In 1619, the new "Town of Berkeley Hundred and Plantation" was established. Within a few years it had developed into one of the early communities on the James. This thriving colony was essentially abandoned in the years after 1622, when the Indian Massacre, a planned and concentrated attack on settlers by the Indians, demolished Berkeley Hundred.

In the following century, it became the property of the Harrison family, whose members contributed, in every capacity, to the founding of a new nation: attorney generals, Speakers of the House of Burgesses, Treasurers of the Colony of Virginia, signers of The Declaration of Independence and Presidents of the United States.

The house at Berkeley is handsome — a Georgian beauty with two flanking dependencies. One was used as a laundry and kitchen and the other was used as a schoolhouse for the children of the family. One of the most fascinating features of Berkeley is one which was discovered by accident: during the restoration of the house some years ago, the plaster was removed from the wall of one of the drawing rooms, and the signature of Benjamin Harrison IV, who altered the house, was uncovered. The original date stone is on the western side of the manor house, and is inscribed with the date 1726.

The main house at Berkeley actually has four floors. The basement is English, partially above ground, and within it is the arched brick construction which supports this mansion. The first floor is composed of reception rooms. On the stair landing is a musicians' balcony, an opening of the stairwell which is situated to overlook the first floor, where musicians sat to play for 18th century revelry. The third floor contains living quarters, and the fourth floor is a half-story with dormer windows. Many Tidewater Virginia houses utilized half-stories, as the English kings levied their real estate taxes according to the number of floors in the houses. On one of the window panes of the fourth floor is the imprint of a man shaving — a freak of natural photography, achieved by a well-placed, but ill-fated, strike of lightning.

Boxwood gardens border the terraced walk from the plantation down to the James River.

Four generations of Jamiesons have lived at Berkeley. Three are still there and Berkeley is a tribute to one of them. Malcolm Jamieson came to Berkeley as a child, for summer visits to a Southern Plantation purchased by Mac's Scottish father in the early 20th century. Berkeley had scarcely begun to recover from the desecration of the Union General McClellan's Civil War encampment, when Mac's deep affection for this house began. One of my favorite photographs of life at Berkeley is one that is not shown frequently to the public. Visitors see the site of the first shipyards of our new colonies, and the ancestral home of two American presidents. The photograph which I treasure is that of a small boy with a wide grin conquering his first pony — a pinto rearing to child's command, a child, with a good seat, holding the reins. This is so indicative of Mac Jamieson's personality and his intense connection with his home — he simply took Berkeley by the reins. His magnetism and strength carried this house — known as the great plantation of the Harrisons and built by the father of a signer of The Declaration of Independence — and perpetrated it as one of our country's most historic monuments.

Thanksgiving at Berkeley is a time of year to remember. This occurs somewhat earlier than the Thanksgiving recognized in New England. The Berkeley date is December 4, 1619 (from an old calendar) and people from every part of our state flock to this celebration. Tables are spread on the sloping lawns, chairs are pushed near tall green boxwood, and a feast is prepared of turkey, ham, Virginia oysters and candied sweet potatoes. Speeches are delivered, drinks are passed under the table, children run in various directions, and practically every politician prominent in today's Virginia is in attendance.

The preparation of turkey is probably one of the most time consuming of the culinary arts which is connected with this particular event — but the candied potatoes are the dish most appreciated by the local residents.

The dining room at Berkeley contains one of the most interesting pieces of furniture in the house: a gentleman's secretary, tall with wide double doors. It was made in Culpeper, Virginia, for an 18th century man of imagination: within its interior is a myriad of drawers, cubicles, and sections. It is a piece of furniture especially designed to accommodate the needs of one discerning man. Also in this room is a handsome sideboard, from which desserts and coffee are usually served. Over this rests the lovely portrait of the former Grace Eggleston, the very beautiful and gracious Mrs. Malcolm Jamieson.

— opposite —
A traditional Thanksgiving at Berkeley Plantation features, clockwise from top, Baked Virginia Ham,* Roasted Tom Turkey, Carrots and Parsley Potatoes, and Escalloped Oysters.

— below —
Desserts, arranged below the portrait of Mrs. Malcolm Jamieson, are from left, Wine Jelly,* Ambrosia,* Pecan Pie,* Pumpkin Pie, and a Pineapple garnished with Strawberries, Pineapple, and Melon Balls on bamboo skewers.

Brandon

Brandon is down river from Oyster Landing, Sherwood's river frontage, where the early colonists shucked their oysters. If the tide is right, the trip by boat to Brandon takes seven minutes. By car, it takes an hour. Thus it is logical for my husband, Harrison, when he plays tennis with Bobby Daniel, who lives at Brandon, to board his boat in tennis whites, sailing bag filled with racquets and cokes, and take the same method of river transportation, from plantation to plantation, that has been practiced for generations. Bobby is better known as Congressman Robert V. Daniel, elected official to the United States House of Representatives, and his family has lived at Brandon for quite a number of years.

The river approach to this house is spectacular; one first passes the low lands of old Brandon Post Office (mail delivery by water), then the gradually rising fields with dairies, stables and cattle. The boat slows as the land rises, and the gardens of Brandon become evident — acres of formally arranged boxwood, shrubs, lilies, and trees high above the water, with the house in the background. The boat docks against massive pilings of a wooden landing constructed to accommodate ships of ocean-worthy size.

Martin's Brandon was a 17th century king's grant to John Martin, but in 1720, Nathaniel, the son of Benjamin Harrison II, bought 7000 acres and built the oldest part of the present house. His son, Nathaniel, II completed Brandon. This was a common practice — frequently the smaller wing of a great house is the earlier section. The house was within firing lines of both the Revolution and Civil War, and scars of bullets from these times of history are firmly implanted in the walls of Brandon. The formal rooms are paneled in hand-planed heart pine, and the wide hall is spanned by a triple arch supported by columns with composite Ionic-Corinthian capitals. After more than two centuries of ownership, the Harrisons continued to live at Brandon. They served the Colony in many ways: Members of the early House of Burgesses, Councilors, Auditon Generals of the Colony, and as excellent agronomists — with a remarkable amount of acreage under cultivation.

In 1926 the house and plantation were sold. They were bought by the Daniels, a family which has carefully preserved the concept established by the Harrisons: that of gracious living and service to one's state in positions of leadership. The pool house, in the photograph below, contains momentos of one of the present owner's avocations, Big Game Hunting. This building faces the pool, where, on a summer's day, lunch is a casual yet most memorable occasion.

A worldly sportsman's paradise is the setting for a Virginia Game Dinner — Wild Duck Hash,* Corn Muffins, Blueberry Pie and Caesar Salad.

Shirley

Patented in 1613 by the first Royal governor of Virginia and named for his wife, Shirley is a brick Georgian masterpiece whose dependencies form the only Queen Anne forecourt in America. The house was built in the early 18th century, with a lavish disregard for cost. Shirley's stairway climbs upward for three floors with no means of visible support. The walls are elaborately paneled in local wood from floor to ceiling — each room is carved with a different classic design. Incorporated into the mantel in the drawing room were overlapping oak leaves with acorns imbedded at intervals — that was in the 18th century. In the 19th century, inventive Carter children with pocket knives meticulously eliminated all but four of the acorns. In the 20th century, the job was completed by Charles Carter, the nine-year-old, who, with his sister, Harriet, and his brother, Randy, are the tenth generation of one family to live in this house. Charles proudly presented to his parents four somewhat mutilated and ancient acorns. The results of the reception of this gift were not shared with the rest of the family.

The dining room table, Sheraton, is one of my favorite pieces. An earlier Charles Carter, the grandfather of Robert E. Lee, once lived at Shirley. Because of his brood of

— opposite —
A festive dinner in the Carter Dining Room
at Shirley Plantation features a Standing Rib Roast,*
Oven Browned Potatoes, Garden String Beans, Glazed Carrots,
Dresden Sauce,* Spiced Peaches, Dinner Rolls,
and Sautéed Mushrooms.

— opposite —
**An elegant Picnic by the River was an 18th century tradition, and is still enjoyed today on the lawn at Shirley.
Shown, clockwise, are Fresh Baked Breads, Garden Strawberries,* Cold Herb Tomato Soup,* Parsley Chive Butter,* Cornish Game Hens, Watermelon, English Cheeses and Pickled Shrimp.***

— below —
This massive building was the 18th century kitchen and was located a short distance from the main house due to threat of fire.

23 children, who were served formal meals with their parents, it was necessary to have made an elaborate dining table which consisted of several sections. This table still is used at Shirley. Charles Carter transferred dinner (and the table) to the 26 foot drawing room, where Mrs. Carter, who appreciated the value of her Famille Rose and Oriental Export plates, had installed two elegant brass faucets, along the side of the chimney. Sitting at her dining table, with hot water warmed by chimney fires, Mrs. Carter carefully washed her dinner service, while servants refreshed the water and dried the plates.

In the center of the dining table usually rests Nestor's punch bowl. This heavy silver piece is engraved with both the Carter coat of arms and a portrait of Nestor, the famous Carter thoroughbred. Whenever Nestor won his race, the bowl was filled with champagne and taken to the stables to properly refresh this accomplished stallion. These 18th century stables are still in use today. They house 19th century carriages, and at one time played host to my bay mare, a temporary summer resident, who caused some problem by falling into the swimming pool at Upper Shirley.

The silver at Shirley is spectacular. Some of the finest pieces are Britannia Standard. The service, with its large pieces and Queen Anne tray, is always used at dinners and parties. Two marrow spoons are brought out with meats — narrow pieces with elongated ends which are used to scoop the soft and flavorful marrow from the center of the bone. My favorite Carter piece is the ladle, which was made in the late 1700's. Very large and round, six inches in diameter of quarter-inch sterling, this is dipped by its wooden handle into boiling water, which has been filled with local mushrooms. If a poisonous plant is included, the silver immediately tarnishes. If there is no discoloration, the mushrooms are cooked, ladled, and served.

Shirley faces the James. Its double porches look toward Bermuda Hundred, which is across the water. Old City Point, Eppes Island and the Appamattox are to the left. A rare treat is a picnic on the boulder under the large willow oak, a tree that has seen Union ironclads as they barged up this river, Benedict Arnold as he sailed the British Revolutionary ships to Richmond, and Speakers of the House of Burgesses as they returned home to their river plantations.

— right —
The dove cote at Shirley provided many a squab, which was a staple of the 18th century table.

— below —
Shirley's entrance composes the only Queen Anne Forecourt in America.

Hill Carter, a man who fought with his own hands to save his home from being demolished by fire, now lives at Shirley. He has made many contributions to Charles City, both by his long service to the county in a political field, and by his continuing interest in the preservation of its history. His most excellent contribution however, has been his wife, Helle. Born in Copenhagen, Helle combines her keen Danish intellect with our local traditions and the results are spectacular. If one looks closely, one sees Danish pillows, the needlework designed and worked by Helle, quietly incorporated into the very American background of her home.

Helle Carter is one of the most accomplished cooks on the River. Her dinners and luncheons, cocktail parties (and late breakfasts for me when I drop in unannounced) are absolute treats. At small dinners, she usually serves the meal herself, or with the help of her children and one servant. Her cold tomato soup, wine jelly and boiled custard, I recommend to everyone.

Hunting & Fishing

Charles City is a county of seasons. Not Spring, Summer, or Winter, but the Seasons of Crops and Hunting Seasons: bird, deer, fox and goose, and the Season for the Shad to Run.

I know that on the opening day of Hunting Season, no help will show — an understood phenomenon. Husbands, sons, and outdoor daughters leave the house at dawn and return in late evening with quail, duck, goose and partridge to be hung on the side of the wine house to season. Cousins from Shirley, North Bend, Binns Hall, Evelynton, and Sherwood Forest, a distance of twenty miles and thousands of acres, congregate in organized groups in the preferred hunting areas. There is little question concerning who owns what land. These men have shared ancestors and hunting rights for more than a hundred years before Washington was born. There has been little dispersement - and those who have moved away return for their particular season.

Guns are cleaned in the kitchen, feathers line the disposal areas, and boots caked with mud are stacked by the back door. Tales of doe leading hunters away from bucks at the Lions Den, geese that circle year after year and feed on fields at Curles Neck, coveys of quail that fly at Big Buckland, the new stand at Indian Fields — these are the conversational topics. Juleps, scotch and clear vodka are mixed by an open fire in a library which was once the bedroom of a President of the United States, and telephone calls are made to tell worried wives that husbands are spending the night.

Hunting is at its best on a cold, foggy day. Geese fly in wet weather, and the scent of a fox lies low in the cold and rises only when the day's heat carries it upward. Labradors move with webbed feet through marsh grass, and, in distant fields, the voices of hounds are heard on a different line.

It sometimes is disconcerting for me to realize that as I canter on horseback in an organized field, it is possible to glance away from the prescribed pattern of the formal fox hunt and see, leaning motionless against the trunk of a tree, the hunter of a different type — red hat, khaki jacket and rifle in hand — waiting without movement for the same prey as I.

Blood sports are much in evidence in Charles City's country life. It is essential to the propagation of wild life that a proper balance be maintained, and nature doesn't always regulate this. Hounds are bred, season after season, for their nose and voice. Early mornings in the summer, the season of non-hunting and late sleeping, are punctuated at dawn by the sound of Bernard Haynes's and Ashton Yates's hounds being trained. Afternoons are broken by Martin Howard, who stops by to show me his Labrador, a dog trained to hand command for field trial. And sad days are ended with the removal, from our property, of the discarded hounds of the casual hunters, the ones who poach and trespass, leaving in the woods their old hounds to die rather than go to the expense of feeding them another year.

It is difficult to condone this. My pastures have been filled with the animals of other Seasons — Beau, Goldie, Intrepid, and Henry Horse Tyler, those who hunted well but will not hunt again, and a home is provided for their past performances of excellence.

Fishing Season is altogether a different thing. The professional fishermen who ply the James form a great part of its heritage. Most of these men are respected members of the community who pay high taxes for the privilege of sustaining their fykes and nets. Their boats, seines, and fish houses are conducted on the regular level of good business.

One of the deepest points of the James River, Sturgeon Point, is located adjacent to the edge of our property. Here the channel, at 96 feet, moves directly to the shore. In the past century, Sturgeon Point was a center of much activity. Here the fish who produced the American caviar were annihilated in the James — an activity which took

Faded duck blinds, host to the winter hunter, are constructed upon cypress knees, and nestle against the shore line of the James.

no little effort. On summer mornings, the sun pushes upward through the trees from the length of the river. From a mist of haze, I have heard the sound of Norman Haynes's boats for more than a decade. I can tell the time by the sound of his motors. He is an example of the most preferred of the professional river fishermen.

There is also the casual fisherman. This comprises almost the entire male population of Charles City County — and includes residents from the surrounding area of 50 or 60 miles. This activity is not limited to those of an agrarian-oriented occupation, but includes those who now occupy the executive offices of some of the largest firms in Virginia. In early spring, business suits are exchanged for jeans and open shirts, cars are tucked away, and boats and nets are brought out for the shad Season. A week, or possibly two, is missed from the office, and the result is an abundance of deep freezes which have enough shad roe stocked in them to last for at least two meals per week for a full year.

When my children were small, much activity was exercised in the construction of various nets, fish-traps and tackle, for use in the adjoining creeks of Mapsico, Kittiewan and Kennons. The Prime Target was the River Bass, one of the most delectable of fish. This is never good when it has been out of water for several hours, so it is necessary to make a wire cage to submerge in the river for the storage of the recently caught bass. At dinner, the fish is brought to the house in a small tub, cleaned, and immediately put under the broiler. With lemon-butter, salt, large-grind pepper and onion slices, there are few things better. A summer's supper is made complete with the addition of fresh tomatoes right off the vine and lettuce from the garden.

In the preparation of shad roe, a few rules must be observed. Always dry the roe. Wet roe pops. Cook on a high heat, in bacon fat, and flavor with salt, pepper and lemon juice. Turn only once — very carefully; the skin is tender and breaks easily. Roe must be perfectly prepared. If overdone it is dry, if underdone, it is inedible.

The methods of preparing wild game vary. Larding venison is always a good idea, for it is very lean. Marinating is preferred by some. A good, simple method of preparation is to cut the venison into very thin steaks, flour and season it and cook in fat on a high heat — about five minutes. This is the local way. More elegant tables prefer the venison to be roasted, always well done, because the deer has spent a lifetime of exercise in the open.

There are two schools of thought on duck. Always seal the juices in by drenching in gin or vodka. My gourmet husband, Harrison, prefers to split the duck, season it, lay apple halves and celery stalks on top, and broil it — just enough to keep the blood in. I prefer to roast the halves, breast up, with the same seasonings that Harrison uses. We do not attempt to carve duck — we simply serve one half to each person.

The Tidewater terminology of words — and their local pronunciation — is unique. If you ask for a recipe, you may receive, instead, a blank look. The word is "receipt." This area of Virginia clings to its old English pronunciation.

The asterisks found in the captions throughout the book indicate those receipts which have been included in this cookbook.

Game & Fish

HARRISON'S BROILED ROCKFISH

Serve fresh. If kept out of water for several hours they are not worth eating.

rockfish
lemon juice
salt and pepper
butter

Clean and wash fish thoroughly. Dry. Coat with lemon juice. Salt, pepper and butter heavily. Place under hot broiler with oven door slightly open and cook until done, not very long. Serve underdone, rather than overdone.

I like the heads and tails left intact. Not all people agree. This is a matter of gourmet choice. Garnish with fresh celery greens, lemon wedges, and bits of fresh chopped parsley.

MERI MAJOR'S BROILED HERB FISH

fish fillets
large bunch of lemon balm (or liberal amount of lettuce rinsed with water)
mayonnaise, or oil, or butter
lemon juice
salt and pepper
paprika
chopped parsley
small amount of fresh chopped tarragon (1/2 teaspoon per pound of fillets)

In pyrex rectangular baking dish, place the lemon balm, and if you have tarragon, sprinkle it on top of greens. Lay fillets on top, with skin down. Brush fillets with mayonnaise, or oil, or butter, then saturate with lemon juice. Sprinkle with salt, pepper, paprika, chopped parsley, and tarragon. Place in hot oven (500°). Turn oven to broil. Broil for 10 to 15 minutes (depending on thickness of fillets). Turn oven off or down to 250°. Cover lightly with aluminum foil. Let fish set in oven for 10 to 15 minutes.

VENISON PATÉ

Virginians are intrepid hunters and venison has always been plentiful. This recipe in the 18th century was served as a breakfast or supper dish, sliced and fried.

cooked vension
onion
soft butter
mustard
Worcestershire sauce
ground black pepper
salt
crackers or toast

Grind venison and onion. Mix with butter to spreading consistency. Season with other ingredients. Serve on crackers or toast.

WINSTON'S ONE-POT SEAFOOD FEAST

Delicious, festive, and easy to prepare either in the kitchen, on a barbeque grill, or on the beach.

(Recommended serving per person:)
2 small new potatoes
1 ear sweet corn (in husk)
6 small cherrystone clams
6 large oysters
3 large hard crabs
1/4 pound medium shrimp in shell
1 quart water
1/2 cup vinegar

In large steamer, bring to rapid boil water and vinegar. In top of steamer add potatoes, cover and steam 15 minutes. Add corn, continue steaming 10 minutes, then add seafood and steam until crabs are bright red and clam and oyster shells have opened. Serve with lemon and melted butter.

JAMIE MARABLE'S SALT HERRING

Herring are caught in the James during Season, cleaned, and stored in salt as a measure of preservation. Breakfast, with hominy and tomatoes, is their prime time for service.

salt herring
fine corn meal
fat (preferrably bacon)
salt and pepper

Soak for at least one day, to remove salt. Use either the fillet or the entire fish — head, tail and all. Cook the fish longer than the fillet. To prepare, roll in fine corn meal, fry in fat on medium flame. Sprinkle with salt and pepper. These cook rapidly so when an even brown color is reached, they are done.

ROAST VENISON

(10 to 12 servings)

6 to 7 pound leg of venison
2 cups Burgundy or Claret
1 cup beef bouillon
1 medium-size onion, sliced
1 clove garlic, crushed
1 bay leaf
3 juniper berries (optional)
1 teaspoon salt
6 slices fat salt pork

If the lower part of the leg is used, remove the shank bone. Place meat in a large bowl and refrigerate for 24 hours in a marinade of the next 7 ingredients.

Remove meat from marinade and skewer and tie it into a compact shape. Strain marinade and reserve. If meat thermometer is used, insert it in the thickest part of the muscle. Place the meat on the rack of a shallow roasting pan. Arrange salt pork slices over the top. Roast, uncovered, in a preheated very hot oven (450°) for 20 minutes. Reduce heat to slow (325°) and cook 15 to 18 minutes per pound, or to an internal temperature of 140° for very rare, 150° for medium to well done. Baste meat occasionally with marinade while it is cooking. Transfer meat to a heated platter. Remove and discard fat from pan drippings. Strain and serve hot with the roast.

BRUNSWICK STEW

(one gallon)

Brunswick Stew was born in the woods, for it was originally a hunter's stew using small game such as squirrels. This recipe carries a note: "To be made with gumption."

3 good squirrels and 3 or 4 slices bacon (since squirrels have no fat) or 1 hen (if fat, needs no bacon)
about 1 gallon water
4 large chopped onions
1 quart tomato paste
1 quart corn (12 ears, split and scraped, pulp only)
1/2 cup grated bread crumbs
1/2 pound butter
salt and pepper
sugar

Cook hen or squirrel thoroughly in water with onion and salt to taste, until completely done. Remove all bones and chop up meat, remove skin. Add tomato paste. Let boil about 1 hour.

Add corn. Thicken with bread crumbs and butter. Season to taste with salt, pepper and sugar. Add water if necessary to make a gallon of stew.

EMILY'S SHRIMP AND CRAB CASSEROLE

1 pound crab meat
1 pound shrimp, cooked and shelled
1 cup diced celery
1/4 cup chopped green pepper
1 teaspoon grated onion
1 cup mayonnaise
salt and pepper to taste

Combine ingredients and put into a well greased casserole. Sprinkle with bread crumbs and paprika. Bake 30 minutes at 325°.

BELLE AIR RABBIT PIE

one 3-pound rabbit, dressed
2 quarts water
parsley bouquet
thyme bouquet
2 bay leaves
1 cup diced celery in cloth bag
1 1/2 cups rabbit stock
4 tablespoons butter
2 1/2 tablespoons flour
1 cup milk or cream

Cut rabbit into four pieces and place in 4 quart pot. Cover with water and add next five ingredients. Bring to boil and let simmer over medium heat 2 hours or until meat falls away from bones. Bone rabbit and cut into bite size pieces.

Strain off 1/2 cup rabbit stock. In a 2 quart double boiler melt butter. Stir in flour and then add the stock together with the milk or cream. Cook until the mixture comes to a boil and is smooth, stirring constantly with a wire whisk. Add celery from cloth bag and boned rabbit. Season with salt and pepper. Two tablespoons of sherry or port wine may be added, if you like. Serve over batter bread cooked in a ring mold.

NORTH BEND'S SOFT SHELLED CRABS

Soft shelled crabs are a local delicacy, and are available only during the summer months. These crabs have peeled off their hard shell, and the entire crab is edible — legs, claws, and body.

soft shelled crabs
salt and pepper
flour
butter or oil

The crab *must* be alive and moving. Eliminate, with a long slice, the eye and head section — about 1/4 inch. Pull off "apron," and remove "dead man," white lung section over the edible meat. Wash. Roll in flour which has been salted and peppered. Fry in butter or oil until brown. Serve immediately.

BARBECUED VENISON

Barbecued meats are Southern specialties, and this recipe gives venison an unusual flavor.

1 cup catsup
1 tablespoon salt
2 tablespoons Worcestershire sauce
1 tablespoon butter
1/4 cup vinegar
1 onion, sliced thin
1/8 teaspoon allspice
3 slices lemon

Mix ingredients and bring to a boil. Simmer, stirring occasionally, for 10 minutes. Pour over 3 pounds of venison which has been sauteed in hot fat to brown. Roast in a moderate oven (350°) for 1 to 2 hours, turning occasionally.

BRANDON PLANTATION WILD DUCK HASH

- 2 wild ducks
- 2 tablespoons butter
- 2 tablespoons flour
- 1 teaspoon celery salt
- 1/2 tablespoon soy sauce
- 1/4 cup sherry

Cover ducks with water and boil approximately one hour or until tender, saving stock. Chop duck in pieces suitable for hash. In large frying pan melt butter, add chopped meat and remaining ingredients including reserved stock. Simmer approximately 1/2 hour to 45 minutes. Salt to taste. Serve hash with wild rice, cornbread and a green salad.

LAMB OR VEAL CHOPS ALDEN

from "The Williamsburg Cookbook," published by the Colonial Williamsburg Foundation

A dinner in honor of His Excellency Petrus J. S. De Jong, Prime Minister of the Netherlands. Served at Carter's Grove Plantation.

4 loin lamb or veal chops
salt to taste
1 teaspoon black pepper freshly ground
4 tablespoons butter, divided
8 ounces mushrooms, sliced
4 tablespoons onion, minced
2 cups ketchup
4 teaspoons currant jelly
4 tablespoons Madeira or Dry Sherry

Trim the fat off the chops and season with salt and pepper. Melt 2 tablespoons butter in black iron skillet or dutch oven and saute mushrooms for 3 or 4 minutes, stirring constantly. Remove and hold.

Brown chops, turning once. Hold.

Melt remaining butter in skillet and saute onion. Add ketchup, currant jelly, and Madeira or Sherry. Bring to a boil, reduce heat and simmer 30 minutes. Add browned chops and simmer partially covered, 1 hour, or until meat is tender and sauce thick and dark. Baste occasionally. Add mushrooms 10 minutes before chops are done.

HEARTY SAUSAGE CHOWDER

(8 servings)

1 pound ground pork sausage or 1/2 pound pepperoni
1 large onion
3 cups chicken broth (made with MBT packets or bouillon cubes)
1 cup carrots thinly sliced
2 cups potatoes cubed
2 cups fresh mushrooms sliced or 2 small cans
1 1/2 cups (or frozen package) tiny green butter beans
3/4 teaspoon salt
1/4 teaspoon white pepper
1/8 teaspoon fresh grated nutmeg
1 large sprig dill weed or 1/2 teaspoon ground
1 whole clove garlic, peeled, with 2 toothpicks stuck through
add cream to taste

Fry the sausage in a large 3 to 4 quart kettle, mashing and separating in the process, until about half done and lightly browned. Add the peeled and chopped onion and saute until onion is transparent. (If there seems to be an excess of grease, remove some at this time.) Add the broth, carrots, potatoes, mushrooms, beans, and all seasonings. Cover and cook over low heat for 25 minutes.

Stir in the cream and simmer for several minutes until piping hot. Remove the garlic clove. Serve with a dash of paprika on top.

BARBARA'S FRIED CHICKEN

1 frying chicken, cut into pieces
1 cup flour
salt and pepper
Old Bay Seafood Seasoning
oil

Generously salt and pepper both sides of chicken. Mix flour, more salt and pepper, and about 1 tablespoon Old Bay into a medium size paper bag, and give it a good shake to mix the ingredients. Prepare your frying pan with about one inch of hot Crisco. Shake one or two pieces of chicken in bag and put in hot pan, skin side down. Lightly brown both sides. Turn heat down low, cover and cook 45 to 60 minutes. Uncover for the last 10 minutes, turn up the heat, and the chicken will soon be crispy, but still moist and tender on the inside.

Gravy

Pour off all but 3 or 4 tablespoons grease, leaving all the browned crumbs. Slowly, add enough flour to make it thick and pasty. After it has browned and is smooth, slowly add hot water, stirring until you have the thickness you desire. Salt and pepper to taste.

STUFFED TENDERLOINS

(6 to 8 servings)

2 pork tenderloins
2 large apples, peeled, cored and diced
8 dry prunes, cooked and pitted
3 tablespoons butter
1 cup sweet cream
1 cup sour cream
2 tablespoons white wine
salt
white pepper

Slice the tenderloins lengthwise in half. Open and pound flat. Replace top half of each tenderloin. Place apples over one tenderloin. Drain prunes and pull into chunks, and place over apples. Place the other tenderloin over the filling. Roll like a long sausage and tie securely.

Heat the butter in a deep, heavy skillet and brown the tenderloin slightly. Add the creams, wine and seasonings to taste and cook slowly, covered, for 1 1/2 hours.

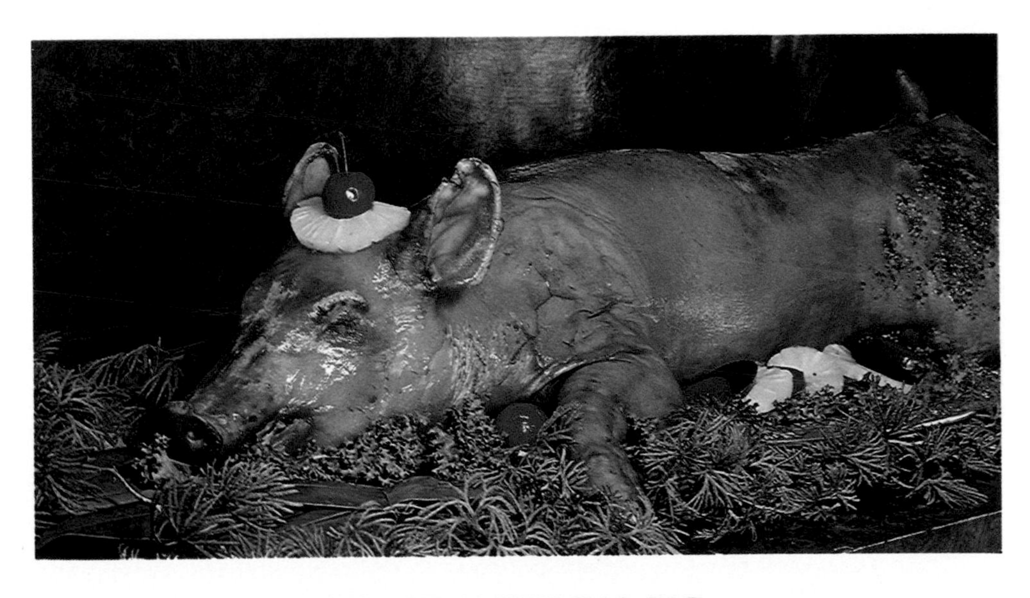

ROAST SUCKLING PIG

Use a very small pig, the younger the better (be careful that it will fit in your oven). Wash thoroughly in cold water. Rub inside cavity with salt and pepper and fill with your favorite poultry stuffing and sew up opening. Roast in 350° oven for 3 to 4 hours. Garnish with crab apples and running cedar.

SHERWOOD FOREST BAKED VIRGINIA HAM

one ham
brown sugar
cloves
orange juice, pear juice, or pineapple juice

Soak ham several days, completely submerged, in water. Scrub with stiff brush to remove all salt, smoking sediment, etc. Place in deep cooker on top of fire, cover with fresh water and lid. Bring to boiling point and simmer about 1 hour. Pour out water; put in fresh water. Almost boil — you want to see bubbles roll up from the bottom, but they must not become a rolling boil on the surface. Cover and cook for 4 to 10 hours, depending on the size of the ham, until the bone is slightly loose. Drain and scrub again.

Score. Rub with something sweet, spicy, and sticky: brown sugar and your choice of fruit juice. Place cloves in the scoring pattern. Place in roasting pan, uncovered, in pre-heated medium oven. Baste until brown. Remove until cool, then refrigerate. Serve whole, garnished with apples or spiced pears, and slice as thinly as possible, starting at the small end and working toward the larger end.

STANDING RIB ROAST WITH DRESDEN SAUCE

Rub roast with salt and pepper and cook to desired doneness. Serve with Helle Carter's Dresden Sauce:

1 cup sour cream
1 teaspoon Dijon mustard
1 1/2 teaspoons horseradish
salt to taste

Mix ingredients until well blended. cover and refrigerate. Serve this creamy horseradish sauce with fondue, fish, corned beef or sliced meat.

BISCUITS SPREAD WITH VIRGINIA HAM PATÉ

from "The Williamsburg Cookbook," published by the Colonial Williamsburg Foundation

(40 regular or 70 cocktail)

1/4 cup French-style prepared mustard
1/2 cup mayonnaise
1 pound Virginia Ham, finely ground
biscuits

Add the mustard and mayonnaise to very finely ground ham; mix thoroughly. Spread on hot biscuits; serve warm.

Note: As an alternative serving suggestion, the ham mixture may be rolled into small balls (about 1 teaspoon) with a peanut in the center, rolled in fine bread crumbs, and fried quickly in deep hot fat until golden brown. Drain well and serve warm.

PICKLED SHRIMP

2 1/2 pounds peeled shrimp, deveined and cooked
2 large onions, sliced into rings
1 1/2 cup salad oil
1 cup white vinegar
2 1/2 teaspoons celery seeds
1 tablespoon capers and juice
4 to 5 bay leaves
several dashes tabasco sauce

Layer hot shrimp and onions in a crystal bowl. Combine remaining ingredients and pour over shrimp and onions. Refrigerate at least 24 hours. Drain most of marinade off and serve with toothpicks.

CHEESE-SAUSAGE BALLS

(about 100 balls)

1 pound spicy country sausage
3 1/2 cups Bisquick
10 ounces sharp cheddar cheese, grated

Break up sausage into small pieces. Mix the Bisquick and cheese and sausage thoroughly and roll into balls about one inch in diameter. Bake on baking sheet at 350° for 20 minutes until golden brown. Serve with a mustard or chili sauce.

SHRIMP DIP

8 ounces sour cream
8 ounces shrimp
2 tablespoons Worcestershire sauce
tabasco sauce to taste
1 teaspoon lemon juice
salt and pepper to taste
1 tablespoon chives

Set aside several whole shrimp. Chop remainder of shrimp. Mix all ingredients, and garnish with whole shrimp.

VEGETABLE BOUQUET

broccoli
cauliflower
carrots
radishes
cucumbers
green peppers
cherry tomatoes

Cut buds of cauliflower and broccoli. Cross cut the carrots. Score cucumbers with a fork and cut crosswise. Make rosettes of the radishes. Stick vegetables on skewers and arrange in a vase.

HAM-ASPARAGUS ROLL UPS

wheat crackers
Smithfield Ham
asparagus spears
pimiento strips

Cut asparagus spears in half. Wrap ham around asparagus. Lay on cracker and garnish with pimiento.

SUGARED NUTS

1 cup sugar
1/4 cup water
1/2 teaspoon cinnamon
pinch of cream of tartar
1 1/2 or 2 cups nut meats
1 teaspoon vanilla

Boil first four ingredients together to form a soft ball — about 5 minutes. Put the nut meats and vanilla into the hot syrup. Stir until they "sugar."

PLANTATION PECAN BALLS

pineapple cream cheese
pecan halves

Spread 1/2 teaspoon cream cheese on a pecan half and cover with another pecan half.

— opposite —
The living room at Berkeley Plantation is the scene for many memorable cocktail parties. The hors d'oeuvres pictured here are, clockwise from the top, Shrimp Dip,* Vince's Cream Cheese Sandwiches,* Ham-Asparagus Roll Ups,* and Plantation Pecan Balls.*

STUFFED MUSHROOMS

- 35 to 40 mushroom caps, 2 to 3 inches in diameter
- 1 large chopped onion
- 1 large carrot grated
- 3 teaspoons butter
- 3 tablespoons minced parsley
- 2 cloves minced garlic
- 1 pound ground veal
- 1 teaspoon salt
- 1/2 teaspoon nutmeg
- 1/2 cup chopped Italian Ham
- 5 tablespoons crushed dry bread crumbs
- 3/4 cup shredded Parmesan cheese
- 3/4 cup chicken broth

Cut the stems from mushrooms and chop. Saute carrot and onion in 1/2 the butter until limp. Add mushrooms and saute lightly. Pour in bowl and mix with parsley and garlic. In remaining butter, saute salt and nutmeg, and add to vegetables with ham, bread crumbs, and cheese. Pack lightly in mushroom caps and arrange in baking dish and pour in broth. Bake 25 minutes in a 375° oven until lightly browned.

VINCE'S CREAM CHEESE SANDWICHES

- thinly sliced pumpernickel
- Smithfield Ham
- breast of turkey
- cream cheese
- sliced black and green olives

Spread cheese on the bread. Place meat on bread and trim excess. Decorate with cream cheese squeezed through a pastry tube, and garnish with sliced olives.

Fresh strawberries with a garnish of garden marigolds. A silver bowl. Simplicity of taste and enjoyment.

TOMATO SOUP WITH HERBS

(1 1/2 quarts)

6 cups tomato juice, chilled
2 teaspoons oregano rubbed through a sieve
salt to taste
1 teaspoon basil, rubbed through a sieve
1/2 teaspoon pepper
1 cup sour cream

Combine all ingredients and blend very well. Chill for at least 4 hours, or overnight, to allow flavors to develop. Garnish with either chopped chives or watercress.

CRAB SOUP

This old fashioned Crab Soup is a favorite.

1 quart milk
small piece of onion
parsley, chopped fine
picked meat of 6 crabs
1 tablespoon butter
1 tablespoon flour
1/2 pint cream
1 beaten egg

Boil milk, onion, and parsley. Then add the crab meat. Boil for 5 minutes. Put butter and flour together. soften with the hot milk mixture and add cream, egg, salt and pepper. Boil 1 minute before serving.

SHELL LANDING OYSTER SOUP

1 pint oysters
1 pint milk
3 tablespoons butter
2 tablespoons flour
1 egg yolk

Cook oysters in own liquor till edges curl. Add milk and butter and bring slowly to boil. Make a paste of flour and cold water. Stir in it the yolk of egg and strain. Use this to thicken soup which will be like thin custard. Use low heat and stir constantly as it will curdle if it gets too hot.

PEANUT SOUP

1/2 cup butter
1 small onion, diced
2 stalks celery, diced
3 tablespoons flour
2 quarts chicken broth
2 cups peanut butter
1/3 teaspoon celery salt
1 teaspoon salt
1 tablespoon lemon juice
ground peanuts

In a large and heavy pot melt butter and saute onion and celery for 5 minutes but do not brown. Add flour and mix well. Add hot chicken broth and cook 1/2 hour. Remove from heat and strain. Add peanut butter, celery salt, salt, and lemon juice. Just before serving, sprinkle with ground peanuts.

WESTOVER CHURCH SLAW DRESSING

1 cup sugar
4 teaspoons dry mustard
2 teaspoons salt
2 teaspoons celery seed
1 1/2 tablespoons flour
4 eggs
1 cup vinegar
1/4 pound salt butter
2 1/2 cups cream or 1 can
evaporated milk

Mix dry ingredients in a bowl. Beat eggs together well in top of double boiler. Add vinegar and dry ingredients and cook. When mixture thickens, add butter, stirring constantly. When thick and smooth, cool thoroughly. Add cream or evaporated milk, then beat and refrigerate.

CAULIFLOWER SALAD

(4 servings)

Salad:
2 cups thinly sliced raw
cauliflower
1/2 cup chopped, ripe olives
1/3 cup finely chopped green
pepper
1/4 cup chopped pimiento
3 tablespoons chopped onion

Dressing:
1 1/2 tablespoons lemon juice
1 1/2 tablespoons wine vinegar
4 1/2 tablespoons salad oil
salt and pepper
1/4 teaspoon sugar

4 lettuce leaves

Combine all salad ingredients in bowl. Make dressing by blending all ingredients. Pour dressing over cauliflower mixture and marinate in refrigerator 1 hour. Serve on lettuce leaves.

ENGLISH CHOPPED "PICKEL"

This is an old recipe for an end-of-garden condiment that has many, many variations in old cookbooks. Chop up the vegetables before salting them.

1 1/2 heads large white cabbage
1/2 gallons cucumbers, out
of brine
1/2 gallons green tomatoes
15 large onions
3 quarts vinegar
4 pounds brown sugar
1 pound raisins
3 green peppers, 3 red peppers
4 tablespoons celery seed
6 tablespoons white mustard seed
1 1/2 teaspoons allspice
1 teaspoon ginger

Sprinkle first four ingredients with salt. Let stand overnight, wash and drain. Add remaining ingredients. Boil for 10 minutes. Put in jars.

DILL TOMATO PICKLE

tiny green cherry or pear tomatoes
buds of garlic
stalks of celery
green peppers quartered
1 quarts water
1 quart vinegar
1 cup salt
dill to taste

Wash and pack tomatoes in sterile jars. Add one bud garlic, one stalk celery and one green pepper to each quart jar. Boil brine of water, vinegar, salt and dill. Pour over tomatoes in the jars and seal at once.

BERKELEY MANGO CHUTNEY

1 quart apple vinegar
7 cups brown sugar
2 packages of seedless raisins
10 cloves garlic chopped fine
1 1/2 cups chopped onions
3 tablespoons salt
1 1/2 tablespoons red pepper
3/4 cup root ginger crushed fine

Cook these ingredients in a kettle slowly for 40 minutes. Then put in 10 cups of mangoes which have been cut and peeled. Cook till thick. Peaches may be substituted for mangoes.

ROBERT KEENE'S PICKLED OKRA

small fresh okra
water
apple cider vinegar
garlic salt and table salt
Tabasco sauce
hot red peppers

Select small garden fresh okra. Wash and trim stems. Boil equal amounts of water and apple cider vinegar. Season with garlic salt and Tabasco sauce to taste. Pack okra in jar along with several hot red peppers. Pour boiling liquid over the okra and seal containers. Allow to stand at least 6 weeks.

CORN RELISH

18 to 20 ears garden corn
4 cups chopped celery
2 cups chopped sweet red peppers
2 cups green peppers
2 cups sugar
2 cups vinegar
1 cup chopped onion
2 teaspoons celery seed
1/4 cup sifted flour
2 tablespoons dry mustard
1 teaspoon ground turmeric

Boil corn 5 minutes. Dunk into cold water. Remove and drain. Cut corn off cobs.

Combine in large container (heavy metal) celery, peppers, sugar, vinegar, onion, celery seed, 2 cups water and a tablespoon salt. Boil 5 minutes and stir occasionally. Mix mustard, flour and turmeric and blend in 1/2 cup cold water. Add corn and boil 5 minutes. Pack into pint jars and can as normal.

DANDELION WINE

2 quarts dandelion blossoms (Gather quickly, as they shrink)
1 orange sliced thinly
2 gallons water
3 or 4 lemons sliced thinly
2 pounds sugar
1 pound raisins
2 yeast cakes

Boil blossoms with water, lemon and orange for 15 minutes. Let mixture get lukewarm. Add sugar and stir thoroughly. Pour into 3 or 4 gallon crock. While still warm, add raisins and yeast cakes, crumbled. Stir thoroughly — then cover with top.

Let stand for 4 days, then strain through cheese cloth. Let stand again in crock or large bottles for 10 days, then bottle. (May need to be strained again before bottling, depending upon sediment.)

TRADITIONAL VIRGINIA EGG NOG

(about 24 cups)

Serve from a crystal or silver bowl, dotted with little islands of whipped cream.

1 dozen eggs
1 pint bourbon
1 pint brandy
1 quart whipping cream
1 cup milk
1 1/2 cups sugar

Beat egg yolks and sugar until stiff. Beat in whiskey slowly until blended, then stir in stiffly beaten cream, fold in stiffly beaten egg whites. Thin mixture with milk and allow to ripen overnight in refrigerator.

TYLER'S MINT JULEP

The main ingredients are:

good bourbon
flavorful mint
sugar
silver beakers
one thirsty gentleman

To each jigger of water, add 1 teaspoon sugar. Dissolve. Crush a good deal of mint in this. Add about 4 to 5 jiggers bourbon. Make a generous amount. Fill the beakers with crushed ice, pour in mixture, let ice subside. By this time the beakers should be covered with frost — the pride and joy of the julep — so never touch the beaker during preparation. Add more ice, place a sprig of mint in the side, and serve with pleasure to one happy, thirsty gentleman.

— opposite —
Afternoon on the south porch at Sherwood Forest, where President John Tyler leisurely read his newspapers and served Mint Juleps* to men who were Heads of States.

OLD VIRGINIA SPOON BREAD

(4 to 6 servings)

1 cup cornmeal
1 tablespoon shortening
1 teaspoon salt
1 cup boiling water
2 cups milk
3 eggs
3 teaspoons baking powder

Mix salt with cornmeal, cut in shortening. Slowly pour in cup of boiling water, stirring as you pour in. Beat the eggs in the milk to blend well and stir in, then add baking powder and blend all ingredients well. Grease casserole generously and pour in ingredients. Cook in medium oven (350°) and bake 30 minutes or until brown on top. While baking stir two or three times before ingredients congeal. Serve hot from casserole.

WESTOVER CRACKERS

1/3 cup or less water
1 cup flour
1 tablespoon melted butter
pinch of salt

Roll dough thin and cut with a circle cutter (a ground coffee can lid is ideal). Bake in 350° oven until lightly browned and blistery — about 10 minutes.

BATTER BREAD

1 cup cornmeal
1 1/2 cup boiling water
1/4 cup shortening
1 teaspoon salt
1 1/2 cup milk
2 tablespoons sugar
1 teaspoon baking powder
2 eggs beaten until light

Pour boiling water over sifted cornmeal and shortening. Mix well. Add sugar and salt. Add milk to beaten egg. Then add to other mixture. Stir in baking powder and beat. pour into well greased container. Bake 1 hour at 350°, or 1/2 hour at 400°.

WESTOVER CHURCH HUSH PUPPIES

According to legend, Hush Puppies, were named during the War Between the States. Dogs followed the camping soldiers, and when fresh fish were caught and cooked, bits of corn meal were thrown into the fat and given to the dogs to keep them quiet. The finger sized corn bread was so good that it is now traditional with fried fish.

1 cup meal
2 tablespoons flour
1 1/2 teaspoons salt
1 teaspoon baking powder
3 tablespoons onion, chopped
1/4 teaspoon soda
2 eggs
1/2 cup buttermilk
1/4 cup sweet milk

Sift meal, then sift together the other dry ingredients. Add onion, eggs and milk gradually. Beat well. Drop by spoonsful (dessert size) into deep fat heated to 350°. Cook until brown, and drain on paper towels.

BEATEN BISCUITS

4 cups flour
2 teaspoons sugar
1/2 teaspoon baking powder
1/4 teaspoon cream of tartar
1 rounded teaspoon salt
1/2 cup lard (no substitute), ice cold
about 1 cup ice cold water

Cut lard into dry ingredients adding ice water to make a dry dough. Beat with a hatchet about 15 minutes until a piece of dough pulled off will snap. Flatten dough and fold over as you beat. An old fashioned "biscuit break" will do the beating for you. Roll out to 1/4 inch thickness and cut into biscuits, marking the top with 3 fork prints. Bake at 425° for 10 minutes. Reduce to 400° for 25 minutes. Do not bake too long.

JAMES CHILE'S SALLY LUNN

1 envelope dry yeast
1/4 cup warm water
1 cup scalded milk
1/2 cup butter (no substitute)
3 eggs, beaten
4 cups flour
1/4 cup sugar

Soften and dissolve yeast in water. Dissolve and mix butter, milk and sugar by stirring over medium heat. Cool. Combine yeast, milk mixture and eggs. Beat until smooth with a wooden spoon. Add enough flour to make soft batter. Beat until very elastic. Put in large bowl, cover with damp cloth. Let rise until double in size. (About 60 minutes.) Knock down and beat until smooth. Place in a greased 2 quart mold. Cover with cloth, let rise again until size doubles. (About 3/4 hour.)

Bake in oven preheated at 325° for about 3/4 hour. Serve hot with butter. Slice as you would a cake and serve so that it looks uncut and whole.

PARSLEY-CHIVES BREAD

french bread or sour dough bread
1 stick butter
3 tablespoons parsley, chopped fine
3 tablespoons chive, chopped fine

Mix butter, parsley, and chives and let set for 24 hours. Spread on thinly sliced bread. Serve cold.

RUSKS

1 fresh yeast cake
1 cup scalded milk
1/2 cup shortening
2 well beaten eggs
flavoring as desired
2 cups flour, or enough to make stiff dough
1 1/2 cups sugar
1 tablespoon ground ginger

Make sponge of first 6 ingredients. Let rise until doubled in bulk. Add 1 cup sugar, then form into biscuit shapes and let rise again. Mix 1/2 cup sugar with ground ginger, moisten with water, and spread on top of each rusk. Bake slowly.

GRACE JAMIESON'S MUSHROOMS AND WATERCRESS IN SOUR CREAM

At Berkeley today the Malcolm Jamiesons entertain frequently and with a flair for the unusual. Virginia's old fashioned foods take on a new interest and continental flavor.

1 stick butter
small clove garlic, minced
4 cups fresh mushrooms
2 bunches watercress
dash cooking sherry
1 tablespoon lemon juice
1 cup thick sour cream

Melt butter in a saucepan. Add garlic, and sliced mushrooms, unpeeled. If unable to get them, use two 6 ounce cans. Simmer mixture slowly for 15 minutes. Then add chopped watercress, tops only, and lemon juice. Continue to simmer 20 more minutes. Then slowly blend in sour cream. Let heat a few minutes and serve on small pieces of crisp toast.

ZUCCHINI WITH TOMATOES AND PEPPERS

Onions may be used instead of peppers, if desired

6 medium zucchini, quartered and in 1/2 inch slices
4 medium tomatoes, cut into half quarters (8 slices per tomato)
2 peppers, sliced lengthwise
1/4 teaspoon oregano
1/2 teaspoon salt
1/4 teaspoon white pepper

Mix all ingredients. Put in a casserole dish. Dot with 2 tablespoons butter. Bake at 350° for 1 1/2 hours.

BELLE AIR CORN PUDDING

4 cups white corn, fresh or canned
2 large eggs, beaten
3 tablespoons flour
1/4 teaspoon salt
1 cup milk or light cream
2 tablespoons melted butter

Mix all ingredients. Sprinkle up to 1/4 teaspoon fresh ground nutmeg on top and bake at 325° for 1 hour.

SHERWOOD FOREST STUFFED TOMATOES

6 small, firm tomatoes
1 1/2 cups petit pois (tiny peas) or creamed spinach

Cut a pocket in top of tomato. Fill tomato with peas or spinach. Bake in 350° oven for 15 minutes. If using spinach, garnish with finely chopped hard boiled egg.

CANDIED SWEET POTATOES

(4 servings)

3 large sweet potatoes
1 cup brown sugar
1/2 cup water
5 tablespoons butter
cinnamon
orange peel
pecans

Boil whole potatoes until tender. Skin and slice. Place in buttered casserole dish layers of potatoes sprinkled with sugar, pecans, cinnamon, and butter. When dish is filled, sprinkle top layer with same, but add orange peel. Add water and bake at 350° for about 30 minutes.

THELMA'S MASHED POTATOES

6 new potatoes
salt and pepper
butter
1 small onion, minced
3 tablespoons vinegar
milk

Boil new potatoes in salted water until tender. Drain very well. Mash potatoes with electric mixer, add salt and pepper, 2 tablespoons butter, onion, 3 tablespoons vinegar. Mix well. If more liquid is needed to make potatoes creamy, use the milk. All ingredients in this recipe are approximated. Tasting is the sure way with any good cook.

VIRGINIA POUND CAKE

This is the real Virginia pound cake. For generations it has been served with a glass of sherry to afternoon guests.

eggs	butter
flour	baking powder
sugar	lemon extract

Weigh the number of eggs you want to use and then weigh that much sugar and that amount of flour and not quite that much butter. (If you have a pound of everything else, use a quarter of a pound less of butter). Beat the yolks and whites of the eggs separately. Wash the salt out of the butter. Cream it until it is very soft. Then begin to mix the cake by putting a little sugar and then a little flour, and then a little butter, and then a little white of the eggs into the egg yolks. (Put a level teaspoon of baking powder into the flour). Continue to add a little of each until all ingredients are in, beating constantly. After beating until smooth, add lemon. Bake in a tube pan lined with brown paper in a 325° oven.

ELIZABETH BAGBY'S OLD FASHIONED CHESS PIE

1/2 pound melted butter	5 eggs, beaten
3/4 pound sugar	3 lemons, juice and grated rind

Mix ingredients together. Bake in small pastry shells, about 2 tablespoons in each, depending on size of tins. Bake at 425° for about 13 minutes, or until lightly browned.

TYLER PUDDING

This recipe was such a favorite with President Tyler that it carries his name. This pudding is a pie for it is baked on a pastry, and one fourth of the recipe is sufficient for a smaller family.

1 fresh coconut, grated	1 cup of thick cream
6 large eggs	1/2 cup butter
5 cups of sugar	pie pastry, uncooked

Cream butter and sugar. Add eggs, well-beaten, then add the cream and last the coconut. Pour into four pie pans (9 inch). Place in preheated 300° oven and bake for 15 or 20 minutes (or until done).

WESTOVER APPLE FLOAT

4 egg whites	1 tablespoon lemon juice
1 quart applesauce, sweetened to taste	nutmeg to taste

Beat egg whites until stiff. Combine other ingredients and fold egg whites into the mixture. Chill before serving.

OLD ENGLISH PLUM PUDDING

1/2 pound beef suet (grated)
2 ounces flour
1/2 pound raisins
1/2 pound sultanas
1/4 pound currants
1/2 nutmeg (grated)
1/2 ounce ground cinnamon
pinch of allspice
pinch of salt
1/4 pound mixed peel
1/2 pound bread crumbs (fine)
2 ounces coconut (shredded)
1 cup milk
1 wine glass rum or brandy
1 lemon (strain juice, grate rind)
4 eggs

Mix all ingredients well together. Put in greased bowl, cover tightly, and steam for 6 hours. Serve with hard sauce: Brown sugar mixed with brandy.

BELLE AIR PLANTATION CARAMEL GINGER PIE

2 large or 3 small eggs
1 cup light brown sugar
2 tablespoons melted butter
1 teaspoon vanilla, or
  2 teaspoons creme de cocoa
1 tablespoon cold water
pinch salt
3 tablespoons crystalized ginger,
  finely chopped

Preheat oven to 150°. Have thin raw pie crust in 9 inch pie pan. Beat eggs. Add sugar and beat again. Beat in the butter, vanilla, water and salt. Stir in ginger. Pour mixture into crust. Bake at 450° for 10 minutes and let sit in oven for another 15 to 20 minutes until "set."

SHIRLEY GINGER SNAPS

3 pounds flour
1 pound butter
1 pound sugar
1 pint molasses
1 teacup ginger
2 teaspoons cinnamon
1/2 teaspoon red pepper

Roll very thin, bake quickly. These are quite hot, but delicious.

WESTOVER CHOCOLATE SOUFFLE

1 1/2 ounces unsweetened
  chocolate
1/3 cup sugar
2 tablespoons hot water
2 tablespoons butter
2 tablespoons flour
3/4 cup milk
1/4 teaspoon salt
3 egg yolks, beaten until thick
3 egg whites
1/2 teaspoon vanilla

Melt chocolate in double boiler. Add water and 1/2 of sugar portion. Melt butter in separate pan. Add flour. Blend the two and then add milk. Stir and cook until it reaches the boiling point. Add chocolate mixture and then salt. Then add egg yolks and let mixture cool. Then in separate bowl beat the 3 egg whites, adding remainder of sugar portion. Fold stiff egg whites into chocolate mixture. Add salt and vanilla.

Turn entire mixture into 2 quart pyrex dish and place pyrex dish in frying pan (or another large oven dish) containing 1 cup (more or less) of water. Put this in oven preheated to 325° and bake for 30 to 40 minutes in a quiet kitchen. Serve this hot, with a very liberal amount of whipped cream as a side dish to be used as a sauce.

"SHIRLEY" WINE SAUCE

On the mahogany sideboard in the dining room at Shirley, rests the silver saucepan in which this Wine Sauce always has been made. The Carters used the sauce for puddings or dumplings, and it added considerably to winter-time desserts.

1/2 pound butter
10 tablespoons brown sugar
yolks of 2 eggs
10 wineglasses of wine
1 glass brandy

Cream butter with brown sugar and the egg yolks. Add wine and brandy. Boil 5 minutes in the silver saucepan.

BERKELEY PECAN PIE

3 eggs, slightly beaten
1 cup sugar
1 cup light corn syrup
pinch cinnamon
1/8 teaspoon salt
1/2 to 1 cup pecan pieces
1 teaspoon vanilla
9 inch unbaked pie shell

Mix the ingredients, adding the nuts last. Pour into 9 inch shallow pie pan lined with pastry, or into a 9 inch unbaked pie shell. Bake at 450° for 10 minutes. Reduce the heat to 325° and bake till filing is firm. (Old timers shook the pie slightly, and when its center remained still, the pie was cooked.) Baking time is about 50 minutes. When done, the top will be firm and crusty with the pecans showing.

Plantation desserts are displayed in the garden at Westover house. Pictured clockwise from the bottom left are Pecan Pie,* Westover Apple Float,* Cherry Pie, Walnut Cake, Apple Dumplings,* and Cheesecake.

BAKED APPLE DUMPLINGS

2 cups flour
4 teaspoons baking powder
1/2 teaspoon salt
2 tablespoons sugar
3/4 cup milk
1/2 cup shortening
6 apples, peeled and cored
1 cup sugar
1 cup water
1 tablespoon butter

Mix flour, baking powder, salt and two tablespoons sugar. Work in shortening with tips of fingers and add milk quickly. Toss on floured board, roll and cut in six inch squares. Place an apple on each, with one tablespoon sugar. Bring up corners, twist and pinch together, and place side by side in a well greased pan. Pour over water and remaining sugar and bake in a hot oven about 45 minutes until crisp and well done. Serve hot with sauce in pan or brandy sauce.

Brandy Sauce

1/2 cup butter
1 cup sugar
1 egg
brandy to taste

Cream butter with sugar. Stir over hot water till the butter and sugar blend and melt. Beat egg with a little water. Add to butter and sugar and stir until thick. Then add brandy to flavor.

AUNT LUCY'S FAT PIE

1 cup sugar
1 cup butter
1 cup damson preserves
yolks of 5 eggs (reserve whites for your favorite meringue topping)

Cream butter. Add sugar and mix well. Add beaten yolks and then the preserves. Place in an uncooked pie shell. Place baking sheet under pie pan, as filling tends to bubble over. Bake in a moderate oven (350°) until crust is evenly browned (about 1 hour). Allow to cool before adding a meringue topping.

HELLE CARTER'S WINE JELLY

2 envelopes gelatin
1 cup cold water
1 cup sugar
1 cup boiling water
1 cup sherry (Port or Maderia)
juice of 1 lemon
whipped cream or Custard Sauce

Soak gelatin in cold water. Dissolve sugar and gelatin mixture in boiling water. Add wine and strained lemon juice. Pour into molds or bowl and chill. Serve with whipped cream or Custard Sauce.

Custard Sauce

1 1/2 tablespoons cornstarch
2 cups light cream
yolks of 4 eggs
1/2 cup sugar
1 teaspoon vanilla

Beat egg yolks until light, then combine with cornstarch dissolved in 1/4 cup of the cream. Heat the remaining cream, but do not boil. Add sugar. While stirring constantly, pour 1 cup of the hot cream/sugar mixture over the egg mixture. Return remaining cream to low heat, then stir in cream and egg mixture. Cook 5 minutes, stirring constantly, until the sauce thickens slightly. Blend in vanilla thoroughly. Serve cold over wine jelly.

COCONUT PIE

- 1 large coconut, grated, and its milk
- 4 eggs
- 3 cups sugar
- 3 tablespoons melted butter
- pastry for a one-crust pie

Beat eggs, add other ingredients. Line pie plate with pastry and bake at 400° for 7 to 10 minutes. Add filling and bake at 450° for 15 minutes. Then reduce temperature to 350° for 35 minutes.

AMBROSIA

Ambrosia was a dessert for special occasions, because of the scarcity of fresh fruits.

- oranges
- pineapple
- grapefruit
- bananas
- tangerines
- granulated sugar
- grated fresh coconut
- strawberries
- sherry

With a sharp knife section citrus fruit, removing membranes and seeds. Arrange with bananas in layers, sprinkling each with a little fine granulated sugar and grated fresh coconut. Dot the top with whole strawberries. Chill before serving.